BROADWAY FOR TEENS

25 SONGS ESPECIALLY CHOSEN FOR YOUNG SINGERS

COMPILED BY LOUISE LERCH

S0-ABD-525

ISBN 1-423-40120-4

HAL•LEONARD®
CORPORATION
7777 W. BLUEMOUND RD. P.O. BOX 13819 MILWAUKEE, WI 53213

Visit Hal Leonard Online at
www.halleonard.com

CONTENTS

Pianists on the CD: [1] Brian Dean, [2] Ruben Piirainin, [3] Christopher Ruck, and [4] Richard Walters

About the Enhanced CD

In addition to piano accompaniments playable on both your CD player and computer, this enhanced CD also includes tempo adjustment and transposition software for computer use only. This software, known as the Amazing Slow Downer, was originally created for use in pop music to allow singers and players the freedom to independently adjust both tempo and pitch elements. Because we believe there may be valuable educational use for these features in classical and theatre music, we have included this software as a tool for both the teacher and student. For quick and easy installation instructions of this software please see below.

This new software feature allows you to adjust the tempo up and down without affecting the pitch. Likewise, the Amazing Slow Downer allows you to shift pitch up and down without affecting the tempo. We recommend that these new tempo and pitch adjustment features be used with care and insight. Ideally, you will be using these recorded accompaniments and the Amazing Slow Downer for practice only.

The audio quality may be somewhat compromised when played through the Amazing Slow Downer. This compromise in quality will not be a factor in playing the CD audio track on a normal CD player or through another audio computer program.

Installation instructions for the Amazing Slow Downer software:

For Macintosh OS 8, 9 and X:
- Load the CD-ROM into your CD-ROM Drive on your computer.
- Each computer is set up a little differently. Your computer may automatically open the audio CD portion of this enhanced CD and begin to play it.
- Double-click on the data portion of the CD-ROM (which will have the Hal Leonard icon in red and be named as the book).
- Double-click on the "Amazing OS 8 (9 or X)" folder.
- Double-click "Amazing Slow Downer"/"Amazing X PA" to run the software from the CD-ROM, or copy this file to your hard disk and run it from there.
- Follow the instructions on-screen to get started. The Amazing Slow Downer should display tempo, pitch and mix bars. Click to select your track and adjust pitch or tempo by sliding the appropriate bar to the left or to the right.

For Windows:
- Load the CD-ROM into your CD-ROM Drive on your computer.
- Each computer is set up a little differently. Your computer may automatically open the audio CD portion of this enhanced CD and begin to play it.
- To access the CD-ROM features, click on My Computer then right click on the Drive that you placed the CD in. Click Open. You should then see a folder named "Amazing Slow Downer". Click to open the "Amazing Slow Downer" folder.
- Double-click "setup.exe" to install the software from the CD-ROM to your hard disk. Follow the on-screen instructions to complete installation.
- Go to "Start", "Programs" and find the "Amazing Slow Downer" folder. Go to that folder and select the "Amazing Slow Downer" software.
- Follow the instructions on-screen to get started. The Amazing Slow Downer should display tempo, pitch and mix bars. Click to select your track and adjust pitch or tempo by sliding the appropriate bar to the left or to the right.
- Note: On Windows NT, 2000 and XP, the user should be logged in as the "Administrator" to guarantee access to the CD-ROM drive. Please see the help file for further information.

Minimum system requirements:

For Macintosh:
Power Macintosh; Mac OS 8.5 or higher; 4 MB Application RAM; 8x Multi-Session CD-ROM drive

For Windows:
Pentium Processor; Windows 95, 98, ME, NT, 2000, XP; 4 MB Application RAM; 8x Multi-Session CD-ROM drive

BEAUTY SCHOOL DROPOUT

from *Grease*

Lyric and Music by Warren Casey
and Jim Jacobs

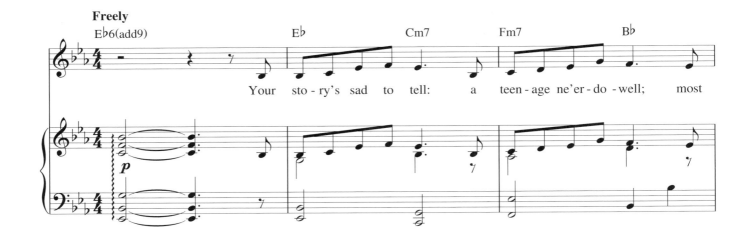

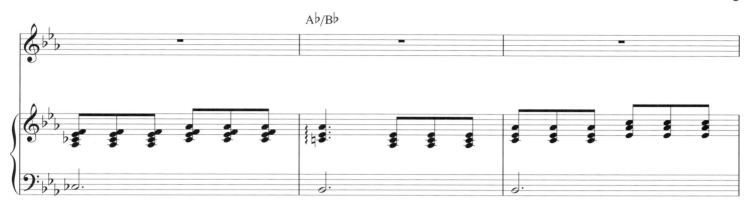

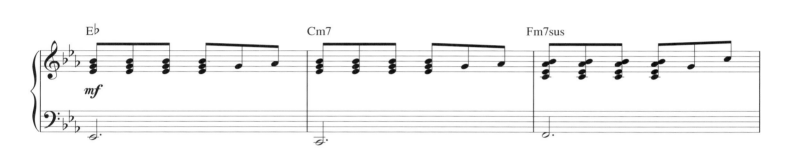

Beau - ty school drop - out, no grad - u - a - tion day for

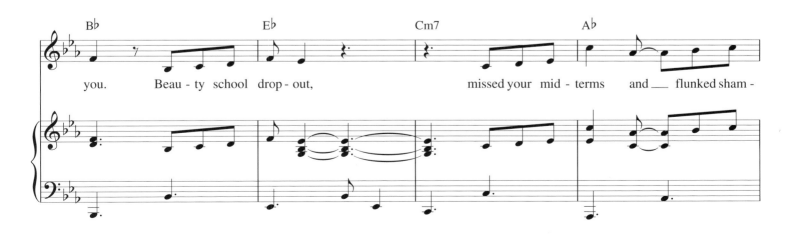

you. Beau - ty school drop - out, missed your mid - terms and ___ flunked sham -

COME WITH ME

from *The Boys from Syracuse*

Words by Lorenz Hart
Music by Richard Rogers

Moderately bright – In 2

Come with me where the food is free, Where the land - lord nev - er comes near you. Be a guest in a house of rest, Where the best of fel - lows can cheer

you. There's your own lit - tle room So

cool, not too much light, _____ Where

you're one man for whom No wife waits up at

night. _____ When day ends you have lots of

friends Who will guard you well while you slum - ber,

Safe from bat - tle and strife, Safe from the

wind and gale. _____ Come with

me to jail. _____

Much slower – In 2

You nev-er have to fetch the milk Or walk the dog at ear-ly dawn. There's no "get up, you're late for work" While you rest in the pearl-y dawn. You're nev-er bored by pol-i-tics. You're priv-i-leged to miss a row of trag-e-dies by Soph-o-cles And

di - a - tribes by Cic - e - ro. Your broth - er's wife will nev - er come On

Rubato

Sun - day noon to bring to you Her lit - tle son, who plays the lute, Her

rall.

In tempo

lit - tle girl to sing to you. You can com - mit your lit - tle sins And rel - a - tives won't

simile

fz   *mf*

yell "fie!" You need - n't take that an - nu - al trip To the or - a - cle at

Del - phi. You snore and swear and stretch and yawn In this, your strict - ly male house. The

on - ly way that sin - ners go to heav - en Is in the jail - house.

cresc. *poco* *a* *poco* *f*

Tempo I

Come with me where the food is free, Where the

mf

land - lord nev - er comes near you.

Be a guest in a house of rest, Where the

best of fel - lows can cheer you.

There's your own lit - tle room, So

cool, not too much light,

Where you're one man for whom No

wife waits up at night.

When day ends you have lots of friends Who will

BEETHOVEN DAY

from *You're a Good Man, Charlie Brown*

Words and Music by
Andrew Lippa

Bee-tho-ven Day! A pol-y-phon-ic jum - ble. A hum-ble ded-i-ca - tion as we

stand up and say: ___ Hoo - ray, Bee - tho - ven, Hoo-ray! ___

Let's im-a-gine it, that glo-ri-ous hour. ___ Filled with e-mo-tion, yet in-

COMEDY TONIGHT

from *A Funny Thing Happened on the Way to the Forum*

Words and Music by
Stephen Sondheim

DO I LOVE YOU BECAUSE YOU'RE BEAUTIFUL?

from *Cinderella*

Lyrics by Oscar Hammerstein II
Music by Richard Rodgers

Am I mak-ing be-lieve I see in you _____ a girl too

love - ly to _____ be real - ly true?

Do I want you be - cause you're

won - der - ful? _____ Or are you won - der - ful _____

CONSIDER YOURSELF

from the Broadway Musical *Oliver!*

Words and Music by
Lionel Bart

Moderate March Tempo

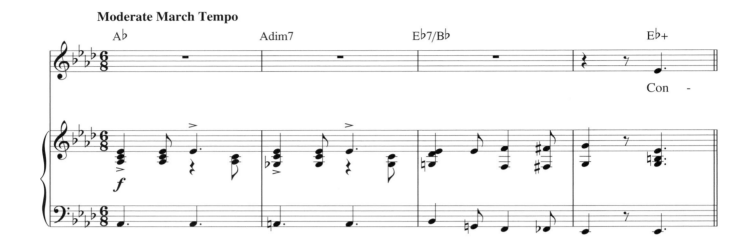

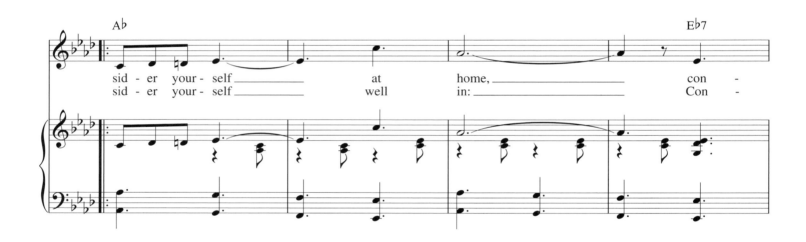

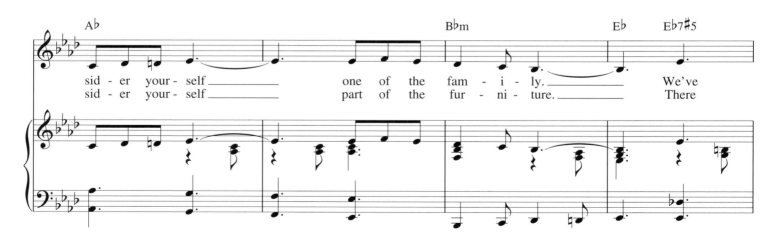

EDELWEISS
from *The Sound of Music*

Lyrics by Oscar Hammerstein II
Music by Richard Rodgers

FROM THIS MOMENT ON
from *Out of This World*

Words and Music by
Cole Porter

THE GIRL THAT I MARRY

from the Stage Production *Annie Get Your Gun*

Words and Music by
Irving Berlin

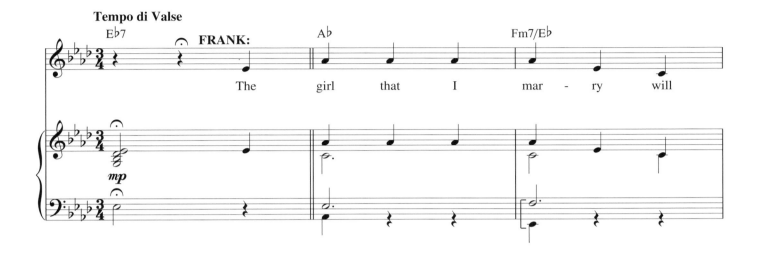

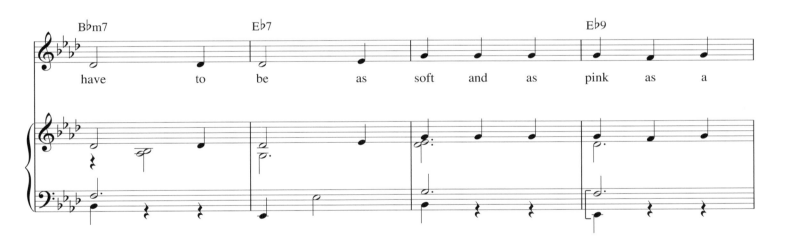

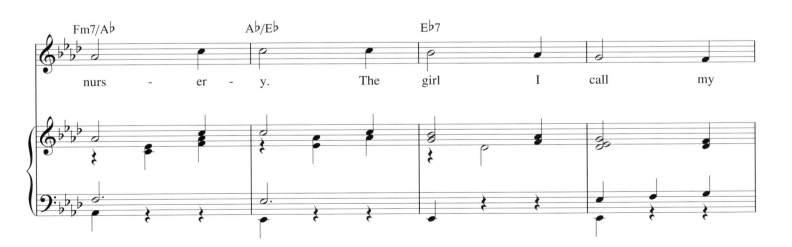

GET ME TO THE CHURCH ON TIME

from *My Fair Lady*

Words by Alan Jay Lerner
Music by Frederick Loewe

I'LL BUILD A STAIRWAY TO PARADISE

from *George White's Scandals of 1922*

Words by B.G. DeSylva and Ira Gershwin
Music by George Gershwin

Moderately

All you preach-ers who de-light in pan-ning the danc-ing teach-ers let me tell you there are a lot of fea-tures of the dance that car-ry you through the gates of Heav-en.

I'M NOT WEARING
UNDERWEAR TODAY

from the Broadway Musical *Avenue Q*

Music and Lyrics by Robert Lopez
and Jeff Marx

For more info about *Avenue Q*, visit www.AvenueQ.com

ISN'T THIS A LOVELY DAY
(to Be Caught in the Rain?)
from the RKO Radio Motion Picture *Top Hat*

Words and Music by
Irving Berlin

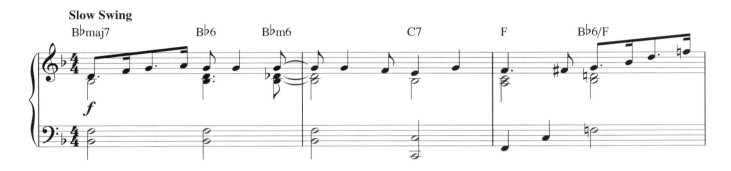

The weath-er is fright-'ning, the thun-der and light-'ning

seem to be hav-ing their way. But as far as I'm con-

I'VE NEVER BEEN IN LOVE BEFORE

from *Guys and Dolls*

By Frank Loesser

IT ONLY TAKES A MOMENT

from *Hello, Dolly!*

Words and Music by
Jerry Herman

NEVER THE LUCK

from *The Mystery of Edwin Drood*

Words and Music by
Rupert Holmes

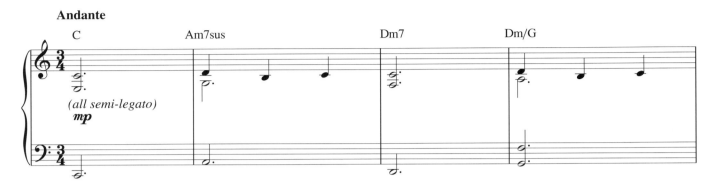

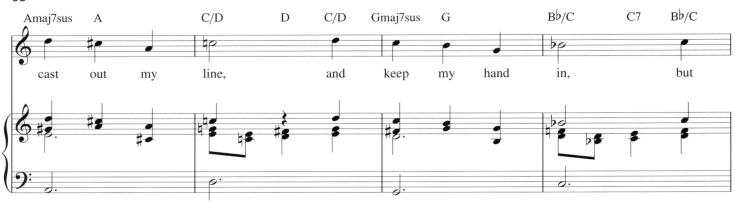

cast out my line, and keep my hand in, but

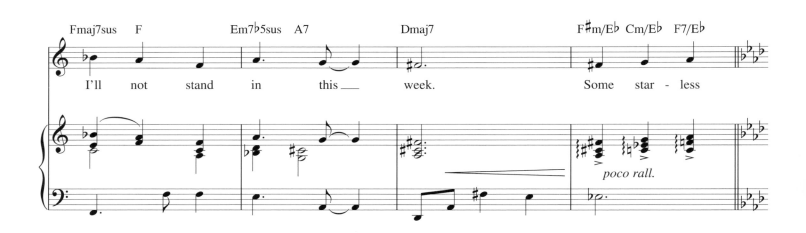

I'll not stand in this___ week. Some star-less

Waltz

night, they'll call t'wards the wings,

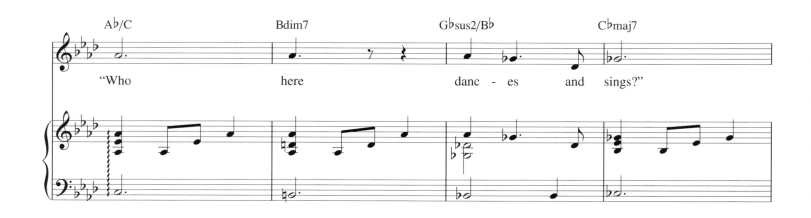

"Who here danc-es and sings?"

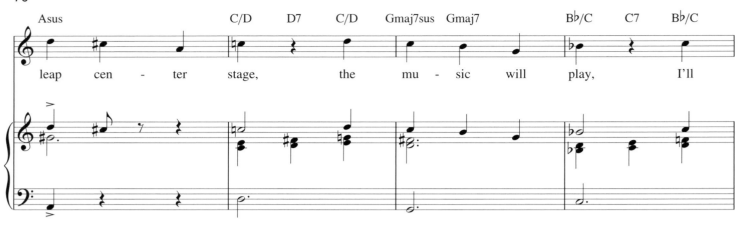

leap cen - ter stage, the mu - sic will play, I'll

waltz my way in - to your heart.

Maestoso

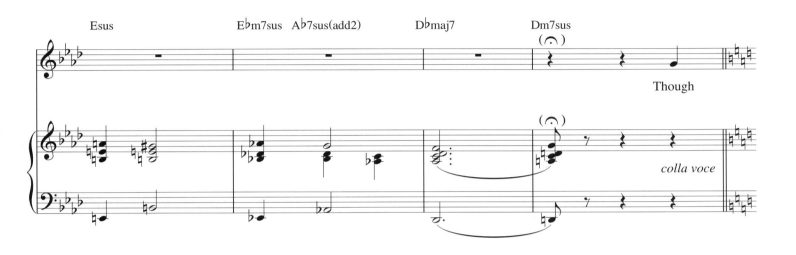

Though

colla voce

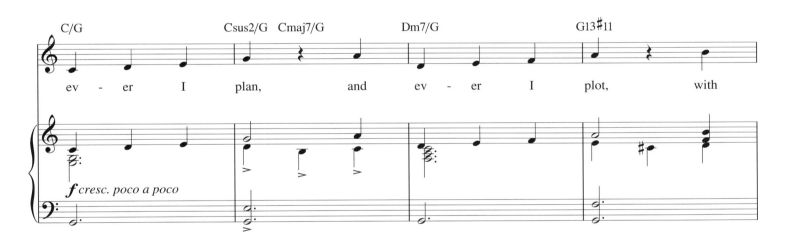

ev - er I plan, and ev - er I plot, with

f *cresc. poco a poco*

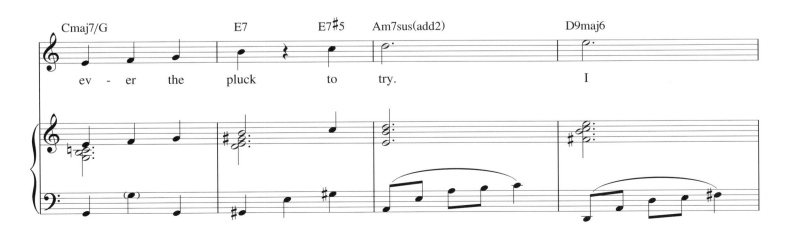

ev - er the pluck to try. I

OH, WHAT A BEAUTIFUL MORNIN'

from *Oklahoma!*

Lyrics by Oscar Hammerstein II
Music by Richard Rodgers

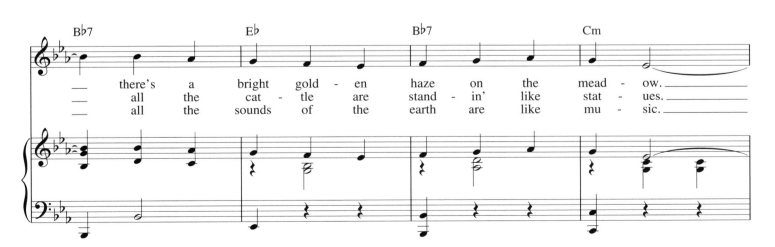

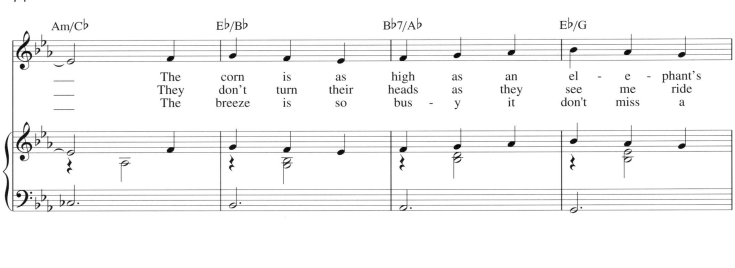

The corn is as high as an el - e - phant's
They don't turn their heads as they see me ride
The breeze is so bus - y it don't miss a

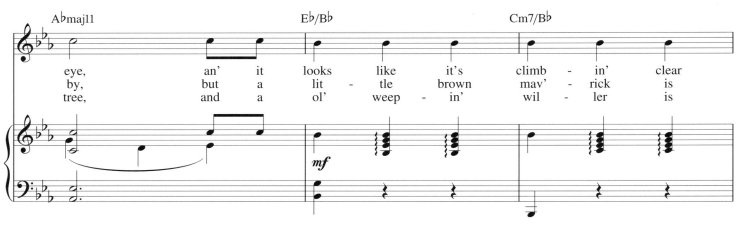

eye, an' it looks like it's climb - in' clear
by, but a lit - tle brown mav' - rick is
tree, and a ol' weep - in' wil - ler is

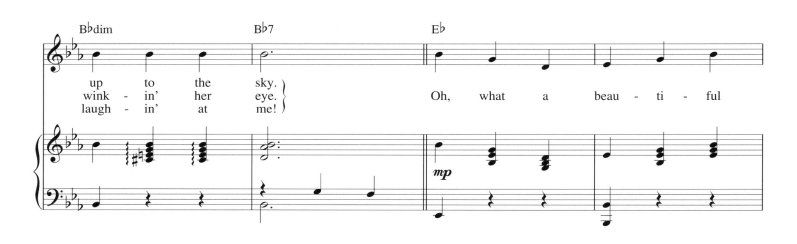

up to the sky.
wink - in' her eye. Oh, what a beau - ti - ful
laugh - in' at me!

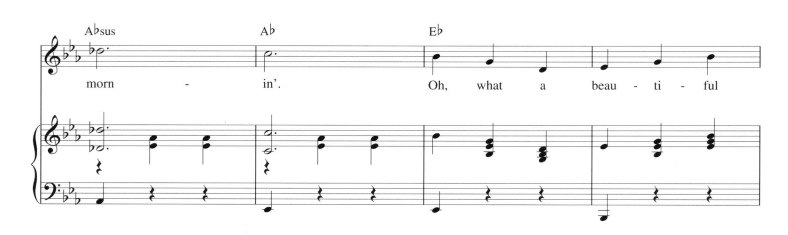

morn - in'. Oh, what a beau - ti - ful

OLD DEVIL MOON

from *Finian's Rainbow*

Words by E.Y. Harburg
Music by Burton Lane

ON THIS NIGHT OF A THOUSAND STARS

from *Evita*

Words by Tim Rice
Music by Andrew Lloyd Webber

Tempo di Tango

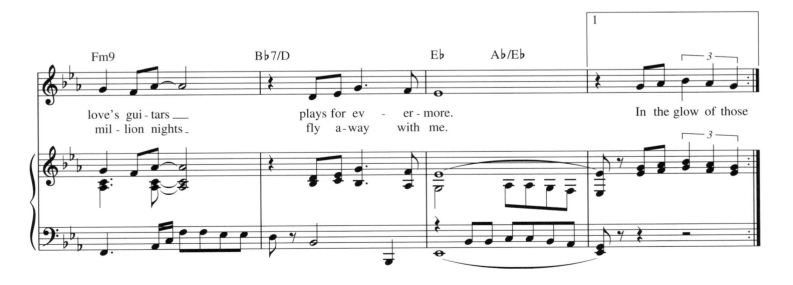

A PRETTY GIRL IS LIKE A MELODY

from the 1919 Stage Production *Ziegfeld Follies*

Words and Music by
Irving Berlin

Moderately (straight eighths)

PUT ON A HAPPY FACE

from *Bye Bye Birdie*

Lyric by Lee Adams
Music by Charles Strouse

STARS

from *Les Misérables*

Music by Claude-Michel Schönberg
Lyrics by Herbert Kretzmer and Alain Boublil

face, till we come face to face. He knows his way in the

dark, but mine is the way of the Lord. And those who fol- low the

path of the right-eous shall have their re - ward. And if they

fall as Lu-ci-fer fell, the flame, _____ the sword!

pay _____ the price. _____

Lord, let me find him, _____ that I may see him _____ safe be-hind

bars! _____ I will nev-er rest _____ 'til then. _____ This I

swear! This I swear by the stars. _____

THERE IS NOTHIN' LIKE A DAME
from *South Pacific*

Lyrics by Oscar Hammerstein II
Music by Richard Rodgers

THIS CAN'T BE LOVE

from *The Boys from Syracuse*

Words by Lorenz Hart
Music by Richard Rodgers

THIS IS THE MOMENT
from *Jekyll & Hyde*

Words by Leslie Bricusse
Music by Frank Wildhorn

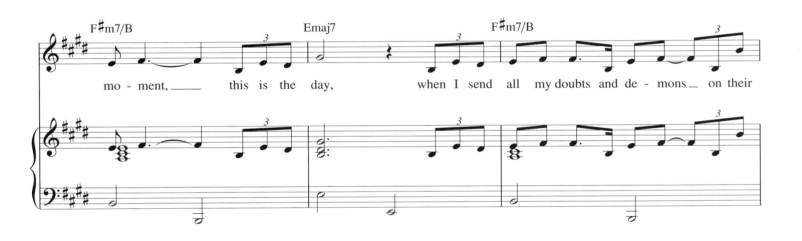

com - ing ____ in - to play, is here and now ___ to - day. ____ This is the

mo - ment, _____ this is the time when the mo - men - tum and the mo - ment are in

rhyme. Give me this mo - ment, _____ this ___ pre - cious chance. I'll

gath - er ____ up my past and make some sense ___ at last. This is the

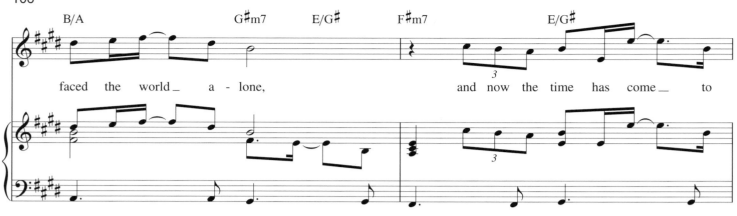

faced the world _ a - lone, and now the time has come _ to

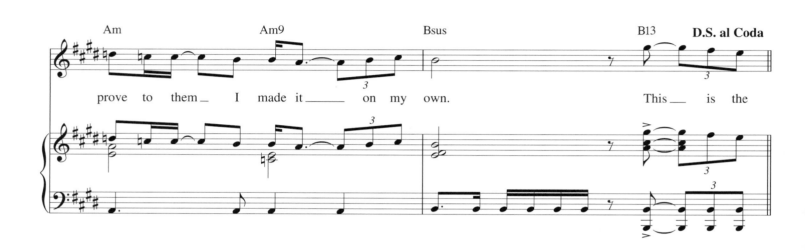

prove to them _ I made it _ on my own. This _ is the

CODA

mo - ment, the sweet-est mo - ment of them all! This is the

mo - ment. Damn all the odds. This day or

MUSICAL THEATRE COLLECTIONS FOR SINGERS

THE ACTOR'S SONG BOOK

A wonderfully diverse collection of comedy songs, character songs, Vaudeville numbers, dramatic songs, and ballads for the actor who sings. A perfect resource for finding an audition piece or specialty number. Two editions, one for women and one for men, with a completely different selection of over 50 songs in each.

00747035 Women's Edition $19.95
00747034 Men's Edition $19.95

THE AUDITION SUITE

FOUR COMIC SONGS FOR THEATRE SINGERS
Lyrics by Martin Charnin
Music by Michael Dansicker
Best known as the lyricist/director for *Annie*, Broadway guru Martin Charnin conceived of this clever collection after noticing a sorry lack of comic songs while auditioning thousands of actors. Featuring his witty words set to the music of accompanist and composer Michael Dansicker, these four funny audition pieces will put smiles on directors' faces – and hopefully land actors roles! The songs are arranged for voice with piano accompaniment and include: Audition 101 • Confession • Family Tree • Special Skills.
00740184 Vocal/Piano $7.95

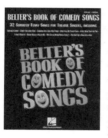

THE BELTER'S BOOK OF COMEDY SONGS

32 SERIOUSLY FUNNY SONGS FOR THEATRE SINGERS
This fabulous collection for women theatre singers includes piano/vocal arrangements in appropriately low belting keys of 32 songs to keep audiences laughing: Adelaide's Lament • Always a Bridesmaid • Dance: Ten; Looks: Three • Diamonds Are a Girl's Best Friend • Don't Call Me Trailer Trash • A Guy What Takes His Time • It Ain't Etiquette • Take Back Your Mink • Why Do the Wrong People Travel? • You Can't Get a Man with a Gun • more.
00740126 Voice and Piano $18.95

BROADWAY BELTER'S SONGBOOK

A great collection for women singers. All songs have been chosen especially for this type of voice, with careful attention to range and keys. 30 songs, including: Broadway Baby • The Lady Is a Tramp • Everything's Coming Up Roses • I'd Give My Life for You • Cabaret • Memory • and more. 176 pages.
00311608 ....$16.95

CONTEMPORARY THEATRE SONGS

With a companion CD of performances and accompaniments
10 songs from contemporary stage productions, including the shows *Evita, Les Miserables, Nine, Phantom, Jekyll & Hyde, Merrily We Roll Along, Sweeney Todd* and *Evening Primrose*. The companion CD offers wonderful performances by talented artists and accompaniments for practice. Many of the songs have never been recorded apart from the original cast albums.

00740014 Soprano $22.95
00740016 Mezzo-Soprano/Belter $22.95
00740017 Men's $22.95

MUSICAL THEATRE ANTHOLOGY FOR TEENS

compiled by Louise Lerch
A three-book series of large collections of theatre and movie musical songs for teens, with no songs duplicated from the best-selling *The Teen's Musical Theatre Collection*. There are over 35 songs in each volume, with enough variety to keep any stage-struck teen singing for months. Songs range from the classic musicals, to Disney movies, to contemporary Broadway shows.

00740157 Young Women's Edition $14.95
00740158 Young Men's Edition $14.95
00740159 Duets $14.95

MUSICAL THEATRE CLASSICS

With a companion CD of performances and accompaniments
A fantastic series featuring the best songs from Broadway classics. Collections are organized by voice type and each book includes recorded piano accompaniments on CD.

00740036 Soprano Volume 1..................................$19.95
00740037 Soprano Volume 2..................................$19.95
00740038 Mezzo-Soprano/Belter Volume 1 ....$19.95
00740039 Mezzo-Soprano/Belter Volume 2 ....$19.95
00740040 Tenor $19.95
00740041 Baritone/Bass...$19.95

SING THE SONGS OF RODGERS & HAMMERSTEIN

with a companion CD of performances and accompaniments
10 songs, including: Do I Love You Because You're Beautiful • I Have Dreamed • If I Loved You • It Might As Well Be Spring • Love, Look Away • People Will Say We're in Love • Some Enchanted Evening • Something Wonderful • The Surrey With the Fringe on Top • You'll Never Walk Alone.

00740092 High Voice..$17.95
00740093 Low Voice...$17.95

THE 16-BAR THEATRE AUDITION

100 SONGS EXCERPTED FOR SUCCESSFUL AUDITIONS
Compiled and Edited by Michael Dansicker
Professionals in musical theatre often complain that singers don't know how to construct an appropriate 16-bar audition, either in choosing a song or in editing an excerpt. With this new series, that problem is solved forever! Each excerpt has been given a thoughtful, graceful and effective form. An enormous variety of literature is represented, from old standards to movie songs to the latest Broadway and Off-Broadway material. With 100 songs per volume, any singing actor, whatever his or her talents and strong suits, will have many choices.

00740253 Soprano $19.95
00740254 Belter (Mezzo-Soprano) $19.95
00740255 Tenor $19.95
00740256 Baritone/Bass...$19.95

THE TEEN'S MUSICAL THEATRE COLLECTION

Compiled by Louise Lerch
These popular publications are compiled especially for the tastes and abilities of the talented teenage singer/actor. Songs span from classic stage musicals, to "the golden age of Hollywood," to the stage and cinema of the 1980s and '90s. Indispensible for teaching young singers, these book/CD packs also include notes on each selection.

00740160 Young Women's Edition Book/CD $24.95
00740077 Young Women's Edition Book Only........$14.95
00740161 Young Men's Edition Book/CD $24.95
00740078 Young Men's Edition Book Only............$14.95

Prices, contents, and availability are subject to change without notice.

Please see our web site for complete contents listings at **www.halleonard.com**

FOR MORE INFORMATION, SEE YOUR LOCAL MUSIC DEALER,
OR WRITE TO:

HAL•LEONARD®
CORPORATION
7777 W. BLUEMOUND RD. P.O. BOX 13819 MILWAUKEE, WI 53213

SOLOS FOR TEENS
Broadway Songs, Songs from Movie Musicals, and Disney Songs

THE TEEN'S MUSICAL THEATRE COLLECTION

Compiled by Louise Lerch

Terrific songs from stage and movie musicals chosen especially for teen singers. Available as a book only, or with piano accompaniment CDs for practice.

Young Women's Edition
33 songs, including: Beauty and the Beast • Feed the Birds • I Could Have Danced All Night • I Have Confidence • It's a Most Unusual Day • Many a New Day • Out of My Dreams • Part of Your World • Stepsisters' Lament • Till There Was You.
00740160 Book/CD $24.95
00740077 Book Only $14.95

Young Men's Edition
29 songs, including: The Bare Necessities • Brush Up Your Shakespeare • Friend like Me • On the Street Where You Live • Santa Fe • Sixteen Going on Seventeen • The Surrey with the Fringe on Top.
00740161 Book/CD $24.95
00740078 Book Only $14.95

MUSICAL THEATRE ANTHOLOGY FOR TEENS

Compiled by Louise Lerch

More great songs appropriate for young voices, with no song duplication between this series and *The Teen's Musical Theatre Collection*. The material spans from classic shows to contemporary. Also available with recorded piano accompaniments on CD.

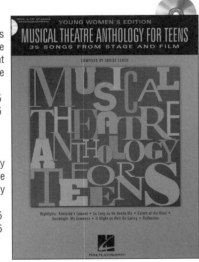

Young Women's Edition
35 songs, including: As Long as He Needs Me • A Bushel and a Peck • Colors of the Wind • I'm Gonna Wash That Man Right Outa My Hair • In My Life • Johnny One Note • Someone Like You.
00740189 Book/CD $25.95
00740157 Book Only $14.95

Young Men's Edition
37 songs, including: All Good Gifts • Any Dream Will Do • Gaston • If I Can't Love Her • Mister Cellophane • One Song Glory • Waitin' for the Light to Shine.
00740190 Book/CD $24.95
00740158 Book Only $14.95

Duets
Includes duets from shows, and also effective duet arrangements of show tunes, for a variety of voice combinations. 30 songs, including: All I Ask of You • Anything You Can Do • I Have Dreamed • Memory • My Favorite Things • People Will Say We're in Love • Sisters • A Whole New World • Written in the Stars.
00740191 Book/CD $24.95
00740159 Book Only $14.95

TUNES FOR TEENS FROM MUSICALS

With a companion CD of full performances by teen singers, and piano accompaniments for practice. The singers on the CD are among the top working young stage professionals in New York.

Young Women's Edition
10 songs: Beauty and the Beast • Goodnight, My Someone • In My Own Little Corner • It Might as Well Be Spring • It's a Most Unusual Day • My New Philosophy • On My Own • The Simple Joys of Maidenhood • There Are Worse Things I Could Do • Wouldn't It Be Loverly.
00740306 Book/CD $19.95

Young Men's Edition
10 songs: All I Need Is the Girl • Comedy Tonight • Gonna Build a Mountain • Les Poissons • My Defenses Are Down • Puttin' on the Ritz • Soon It's Gonna Rain • Waitin' for the Light to Shine • When I'm Not Near the Girl I Love • A Wonderful Day Like Today.
00740307 Book/CD $19.95

GREAT SONGS FROM MUSICALS FOR TEENS

With a companion CD of performances by teen singers, and piano accompaniments for practice. 10 great songs for the aspiring young performer, displaying different moods and vocal strengths.

Young Women's Edition
10 songs: Diamonds Are a Girl's Best Friend • God Help the Outcasts • Honey Bun • I Enjoy Being a Girl • I Got the Sun in the Morning • I'll Know • Much More • Reflection • Shy • Unexpected Song.
00740164 Book/CD $19.95

Young Men's Edition
10 songs: Any Dream Will Do • Close Every Door • Empty Chairs at Empty Tables • Leaning on the Lamp Post • Luck Be a Lady • On the Street Where You Live • River in the Rain • Santa Fe • Steppin' Out with My Baby • Try to Remember.
00740165 Book/CD $19.95

Complete descriptions & song lists online at
www.halleonard.com

THE SINGER'S MUSICAL THEATRE ANTHOLOGY

VOLUME 1

Compiled and edited by Richard Walters

The most comprehensive collection of Broadway selections ever organized specifically for the singer. Each of the five volumes contains important songs chosen because of their appropriateness to that particular voice type. All selections are in their authentic form, excerpted from the original vocal scores. The songs in *The Singer's Musical Theatre Anthology*, written by such noted composers as Kurt Weill, Richard Rodgers, Stephen Sondheim, and Jerome Kern, are vocal masterpieces ideal for the auditioning, practicing or performing vocalist.

SOPRANO – REVISED EDITION

47 songs, including: Where or When • If I Loved You • Goodnight, My Someone • My Funny Valentine • Smoke Gets in Your Eyes • Barbara Song • Till There Was You • Falling in Love with Love • I Could Have Danced All Night • and many more.
00361071 ....$19.95

MEZZO-SOPRANO/BELTER – REVISED EDITION

39 songs, including: Anyone Can Whistle • Broadway Baby • Doin' What Comes Naturally • Don't Cry for Me Argentina • Don't Tell Mama • How Are Things in Glocca Mora? • Losing My Mind • Memory • Send in the Clowns • and more.
00361072 ....$19.95

TENOR – REVISED EDITION

40 songs, including: Being Alive • Johanna • King Herod's Song • Stranger in Paradise • On the Street Where You Live • Younger Than Springtime • Lonely House • Not While I'm Around • Wish You Were Here • and more.
00361073 ....$19.95

BARITONE/BASS – REVISED EDITION

39 songs, including: Camelot • C'est Moi • September Song • The Impossible Dream • Lonely Room • Marian the Librarian • Ol' Man River • Soliloquy • Some Enchanted Evening • and more.
00361074 ....$19.95

DUETS

21 songs, including: Too Many Mornings • We Kiss in a Shadow • People Will Say We're in Love • Bess You Is My Woman • Make Believe • more.
00361075 ....$17.95

VOLUME 2

Compiled and edited by Richard Walters

More great theatre songs for singers in a continuation of this highly successful and important series. As is the case with the first volume, these collections are as valuable to the classical singer as they are to the popular and theatre performer.

SOPRANO, VOLUME 2 – REVISED EDITION

42 songs, including: And This Is My Beloved • How Could I Ever Know • I Whistle a Happy Tune • If I Were a Bell • Moonfall • I'll Know • Take Me to the World • The Sound of Music • Unusual Way • Warm All Over • Without You.
00747066 ....$19.95

MEZZO-SOPRANO/BELTER, VOLUME 2 – REVISED EDITION

38 songs, including: You're the Top • The Party's Over • Adelaide's Lament • I Dreamed a Dream • As Long as He Needs Me • On My Own • I Can Cook Too • If He Walked Into My Life • Never Never Land • Small World • Tell Me on a Sunday • and more.
00747031 ....$19.95

TENOR, VOLUME 2

42 songs, including: Miracles of Miracles • Sit Down, You're Rockin' the Boat • Bring Him Home • Music of the Night • Close Every Door • All Good Gifts • Anthem • I Belive In You • This Is the Moment • Willkommen • Alone at the Drive-In Movie.
00747032 ....$19.95

BARITONE/BASS, VOLUME 2

40 songs, including: This Can't Be Love • Bye, Bye Baby • I Won't Send Roses • The Surrey With the Fringe on Top • Empty Chairs at Empty Tables • I've Grown Accustomed to Her Face • Leaning on a Lamp-post • Lonely Town • Stars • My Defenses Are Down.
00747033 ....$19.95

Note: There is no revision to Tenor or Baritone/Bass Volume 2.

VOLUME 3

Compiled and edited by Richard Walters

By popular request, we've added a third volume to this beneficial series. There is no duplication between any of the volumes.

SOPRANO, VOLUME 3

40 songs, including: Getting to Know You • In My Life • A Little Bit of Good • My Favorite Things • Once You Lose Your Heart • Someone to Watch over Me • There's a Small Hotel • Think of Me • Whistle Down the Wind • Wishing You Were Somehow Here Again • Wouldn't It Be Loverly • and more.
00740122 ....$19.95

MEZZO SOPRANO/BELTER, VOLUME 3

41 songs, including: As If We Never Said Goodbye • But Not for Me • Everything's Coming up Roses • I Ain't Down Yet • Maybe This Time • My Heart Belongs to Daddy • Someone like You • Sooner or Later (I Always Get My Man) • Stepsisters' Lament • The Ladies Who Lunch • You Can't Get a Man with a Gun • many more.
00740123 ....$19.95

TENOR, VOLUME 3

35 songs, including: Almost Like Being in Love • Any Dream Will Do • Corner of the Sky • Hey There • Mama Says • Mister Cellophane • One Song Glory • Steppin' Out with My Baby • Sunset Boulevard • What You'd Call a Dream • Your Eyes • and more.
00740124 ....$19.95

BARITONE/BASS, VOLUME 3

42 songs, including: All I Care About • Gigi • I Confess • If I Can't Love Her • If I Sing • The Kid Inside • Les Poissons • Lost in the Darkness • Lucky to Be Me • Marry Me a Little • Paris by Night • Santa Fe • and more.
00740125 ....$19.95

Prices, contents, and availability are subject to change without notice.

Please see our web site for complete contents listings at **www.halleonard.com**

FOR MORE INFORMATION, SEE YOUR LOCAL MUSIC DEALER,
OR WRITE TO:

HAL•LEONARD® CORPORATION

7777 W. BLUEMOUND RD. P.O. BOX 13819 MILWAUKEE, WI 53213